ZODIAC SIGNS

CANCER

June 22 – July 22

Lydia Lukidis

AV2
www.av2books.com

Step 1
Go to **www.av2books.com**

Step 2
Enter this unique code
FUHPI19KA

Step 3
Explore your interactive eBook!

AV2 is optimized for use on any device

Your interactive eBook comes with...

Contents
Browse a live contents page to easily navigate through resources

Audio
Listen to sections of the book read aloud

Videos
Watch informative video clips

Weblinks
Gain additional information for research

Try This!
Complete activities and hands-on experiments

Key Words
Study vocabulary, and complete a matching word activity

Quizzes
Test your knowledge

Slideshows
View images and captions

... and much, much more!

CANCER

June 22 – July 22

Contents

Are You a Cancer?

Are you an **intuitive** person? Do people say you wear your heart on your sleeve? If this sounds familiar, you might be a Cancer. A Cancer is someone who was born between June 22 and July 22.

Cancer is a sign in the zodiac. This is a series of 12 **constellations** that run across the night sky. For centuries, people have used these groups of stars to tell the future. The study of the stars in this manner is called astrology.

Zodiac Chart

A person's zodiac sign is determined by his or her date of birth. Which sign matches your birthday?

It's in the Stars

The zodiac constellations form a circle around Earth. In one year, Earth makes a full **orbit** around the Sun. As it does this, the Sun appears to be in different places at set times. The zodiac constellations are found along the path the Sun follows.

Long ago, people used the Sun to tell the time of year. In late June, the Sun passed through the Cancer constellation. People born then were said to be born under the sign of Cancer.

Over time, the position of the constellations shifted. Even though the Sun now passes through Cancer at a different time, the dates associated with the sign of Cancer remain the same.

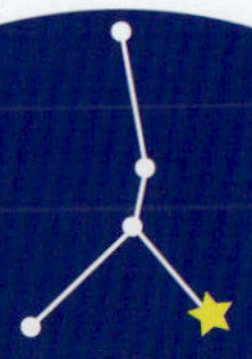

The Cancer constellation is made up of **5 main stars**. The brightest **star**, **Beta Cancri**, is **660 times brighter** than the **Sun**.

Inside the Cancer constellation is a **cluster** of **stars** known as the **Beehive**. It contains about **1,000** stars.

The Cancer constellation is also called the Crab. *Cancer* is the Latin word for "crab."

The Myth of Cancer

The ancient Greeks had stories about how each zodiac constellation came to be in the sky. Cancer is linked to the Greek hero Heracles.

As punishment for killing his family, Heracles was forced to perform 12 tasks. One task was to kill the hydra, a snakelike creature with nine heads. As the gods and goddesses looked on, Heracles began his attack on the hydra.

The goddess Hera did not like Heracles very much. She wanted him to fail at his task. Hera sent a large crab to distract Heracles from the fight.

The crab pounced on Heracles and pinched him hard. Heracles fought back and kicked the crab all the way to the stars. The crab remains in the sky today as the Cancer constellation.

An alternate ending to the myth of Heracles and the hydra says that Heracles crushed the crab and Hera honored it by placing it in the sky. She did not allow the crab to have a bright constellation because it had not defeated Heracles.

Cancer and Cardinal Signs

In astrology, some zodiac signs share certain **qualities**. These qualities show how a person acts in the world. The qualities are separated into three groups. Cardinal signs bring fresh energy to any project. Fixed signs are great at organizing things and putting plans together. Mutable signs thrive on chaos.

Cancer is a cardinal sign. People in this group are always looking for new experiences. They like the rush of new beginnings. These people are also outgoing. They like to be where the action is.

The energy a cardinal sign brings to a group helps motivate people into action.

Zodiac Signs
by Quality

Cardinal Signs
Bring fresh energy to any project.

Aries Cancer Libra Capricorn

Fixed Signs
Organize things and put plans together.

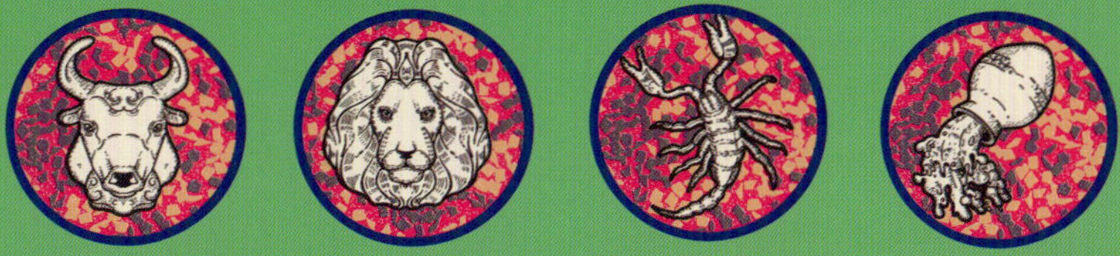

Taurus Leo Scorpio Aquarius

Mutable Signs
Thrive on chaos.

Gemini Virgo Sagittarius Pisces

Cancer as a Water Sign

Zodiac signs are also grouped according to the four **classical elements**. These are fire, earth, water, and air. Signs that belong to the same group share common personality traits.

Cancer is a water sign. Water people are in touch with their feelings. Their emotions often direct their actions. Water people are also very imaginative. They are known to think outside the box.

Water people often express their imagination through creative pursuits, such as painting.

Zodiac Signs
by Element

Fire

Aries | Leo | Sagittarius

Earth

Taurus | Virgo | Capricorn

Air

Gemini | Libra | Aquarius

Water

Cancer | Scorpio | Pisces

Being a Cancer

A Cancer's water traits and cardinal qualities combine to create a specific type of person. A key Cancer strength is **sensitivity**. Cancers are able to pick up on other people's emotions. Their nurturing personality allows them to show compassion when people are feeling down.

Cancers have their weaknesses as well. Their emotions can sometimes get the better of them. They may become dramatic and moody as a result. Cancers can also be insecure. This can lead them to be **suspicious** of others.

The **zodiac** is divided into **12 houses**. Cancer rules the **fourth house** of the zodiac. This house represents **family** and **home life**.

Cancer is ruled by the Moon. The **Moon** takes about **27 days** to **orbit Earth**.

Cancers are considered some of the best listeners in the zodiac. A Cancer will always make time for a friend who needs to talk.

Cancers through Time

Cancers have had a significant impact on the world over time. Some have ruled countries. Others have made their mark in the arts, becoming famous painters, writers, and singers. Cancer contributions have helped make the world what it is today.

336 BC

Alexander the Great (born July 20, 356 BC) becomes the ruler of the ancient kingdom of Macedonia at just 20 years of age.

King Henry VIII of England (born June 28, 1491) marries the first of his six wives. The marriage is dissolved 24 years later.

1509 AD

Poet **Emma Lazarus** (born July 22, 1849) writes "The New Colossus," which now appears on the base of the Statue of Liberty.

1883

1994

Political activist **Nelson Mandela** (born July 18, 1918) becomes South Africa's first black president.

1642

Dutch painter **Rembrandt van Rijn** (born July 15, 1606) completes *Night Watch*, one of his best-known works of art.

2019

Singer **Ariana Grande** (born June 26, 1993) becomes the first solo artist to simultaneously occupy the top three spots on *Billboard* magazine's Hot 100 chart.

Making Friends

Some people believe that zodiac signs can be used to find **compatible** relationships. A Cancer may share more traits with some signs than others. He or she may also have traits that complement those of another sign. Knowing a person's sign may help a Cancer determine how well they will get along with each other.

It's Friendship

Cancers get along well with people born under these signs.

Scorpio

Capricorn

Virgo

It's Love

Cancers often find romance with these signs.

Pisces

Cancer

Taurus

It's Complicated

Libra

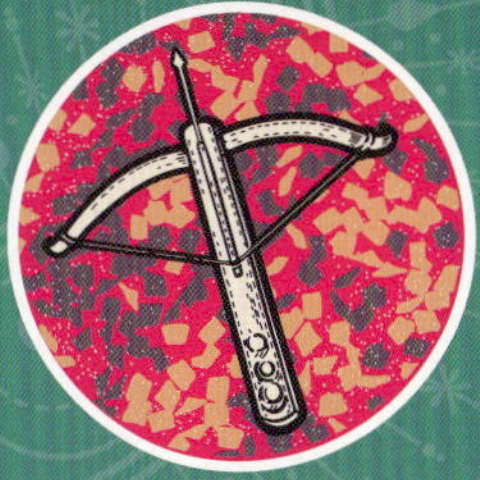

Sagittarius

Aquarius

Cancers find it difficult to form bonds with these signs.

Know Your Cancers

Cancers continue to make an impact on the world. They can be found doing good work in various fields. Did you know these people are Cancers?

Kristen Bell

Born: July 18, 1980

Kristen Bell began acting **professionally** when she was just 13 years old. She caught her big break in 2004 when she was cast as the lead on the television show *Veronica Mars*. Since then, she has appeared in many successful movies. Bell is best known for voicing Princess Anna in the Disney movies *Frozen* and *Frozen II*.

Frozen II is one of the most successful animated movies of all time. It made $1.45 billion dollars worldwide.

Michael Phelps

Born: June 30, 1985

As a child, Michael Phelps was considered a swimming **prodigy**. He competed in his first Olympics when he was just 15 years old, and earned his first world record at the same age. Michael now holds 28 Olympic medals, more than any other Olympian in history. Twenty-three of these medals are gold.

Malala Yousafzai

Born: July 12, 1997

Born in Pakistan, Malala Yousafzai was not allowed to get an education because she was a girl. She felt this was unfair and campaigned for the right of all children to an education. Malala won the **Nobel Peace Prize** when she was 17 years old. Today, she continues to speak out about the importance of education.

Selena Gomez

Born: July 22, 1992

Selena Gomez's first acting job was on the TV show *Barney & Friends*. She was later cast in the series *Wizards of Waverly Place*. Her success on TV led to roles in movies such as *Monte Carlo*. In 2013, Selena recorded her first solo album. She had her first #1 hit in the United States in 2019 with the song "Lose to Love You."

Tom Hanks

Born: July 9, 1956

Tom Hanks started acting in college. After a brief stint on a television **sitcom**, he was given a leading role in the 1984 movie *Splash*. Since then, Tom has gone on to become one of Hollywood's top actors, receiving two **Oscars** and many other awards. One of his best-known movie roles is as the voice of Woody in the *Toy Story* **franchise**.

The Cancer QUIZ

1 When must someone be born to be a Cancer?

2 How many stars are in the Beehive?

3 To which Greek hero is the sign Cancer linked?

4 Is Cancer a cardinal, fixed, or mutable sign?

5 To which element group do Cancers belong?

6 Which Cancer poet wrote "The New Colossus"?

7 What three signs do Cancers have trouble getting along with?

8 What Cancer actress voiced the role of Princess Anna in the movie *Frozen*?

ANSWERS: 1. Between June 22 and July 22 2. About 1,000 3. Heracles 4. Cardinal 5. Water 6. Emma Lazarus 7. Libra, Aquarius, and Sagittarius 8. Kristen Bell

Key Words

classical elements: materials from which all other materials were once believed to be made

compatible: when things or people can exist together in harmony

constellations: groups of stars that form patterns in the sky

franchise: a collection of related films

intuitive: based on feelings rather than facts or proof

Nobel Peace Prize: an award given for achievements in building positive relationships on an international level

orbit: a regular, repeating path that one object in space takes around another

Oscars: also known as the Academy Awards, awards given to recognize achievements in the film industry

prodigy: a young person who shows great talent at something

professionally: as a paid occupation

qualities: traits that makes a person or thing what it is

sensitivity: the ability to understand what other people need and be helpful and kind to them

sitcom: short for situation comedy, a show that places its cast in amusing situations each episode

suspicious: distrustful of someone or something

Index

Get the best of both worlds.

AV2 bridges the gap between print and digital.

The expandable resources toolbar enables quick access to content including **videos**, **audio**, **activities**, **weblinks**, **slideshows**, **quizzes**, and **key words**.

Animated videos make static images come alive.

Resource icons on each page help readers to further **explore key concepts**.

Published by AV2
14 Penn Plaza 9th Floor
New York, NY 10122
Website: www.av2books.com

Library of Congress Control Number: 2020938560

ISBN 978-1-7911-2628-5 (hardcover)
ISBN 978-1-7911-2629-2 (softcover)
ISBN 978-1-7911-2630-8 (multi-user eBook)
ISBN 978-1-7911-2631-5 (single-user eBook)

Printed in Guangzhou, China
1 2 3 4 5 6 7 8 9 0 24 23 22 21 20

062020
101119

Editor: Heather Kissock
Art Director: Terry Paulhus

AV2 acknowledges Getty Images, Alamy, iStock, and Shutterstock as its primary image suppliers for this title.